Power Maths

Year 1 Textb

Series Editor: Tony Staneff

M000111447

Astrid
Astrid is brave.
She loves to
try new things.

flexible

determined

curious

helpful

Flo

Dexter

Ash

Sparks

P Pearson

Contents

This shows us what page to turn to.

I wonder what new things we will find!

How to use this book

Do you remember how to use Power Maths?

These pages help us get ready for a new unit.

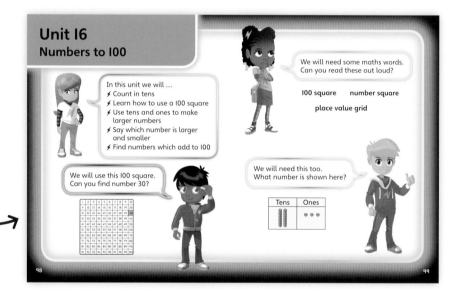

Discover

Lessons start with Discover.

Have fun exploring new maths problems.

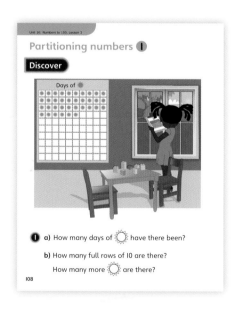

4

Share

Next, we share what we found out.

Did we all solve the problems the same way?

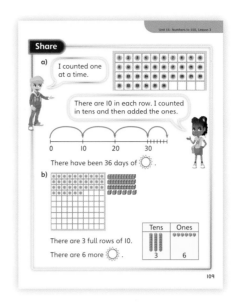

Think together

Then we have a go at some more problems together.

We will try a challenge too!

This tells you which page to go to in your Practice Book.

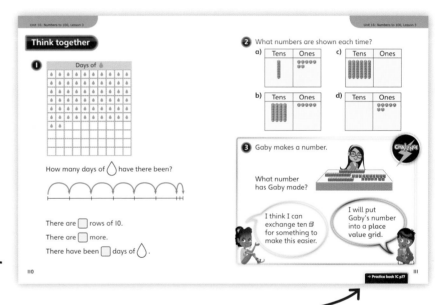

At the end of a unit we will show how much we can do!

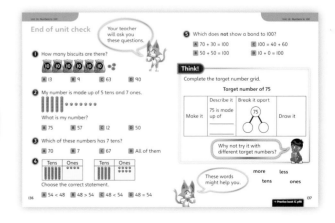

Unit 12
Multiplication

In this unit we will …
- ⚡ Count in 10s, 5s and 2s
- ⚡ Make and add equal groups
- ⚡ Make arrays
- ⚡ Make doubles
- ⚡ Solve word problems

An array will be useful. How many flowers are there? Is there a quicker way to count them?

We will need some maths words. Have you heard any of these before?

equal group   **array**   **row**

column   **double**   **twice**

We will use ten frames to help us find doubles. What is double 3?

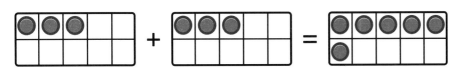

7

Counting in 10s, 5s and 2s

Discover

1 **a)** The class teacher is checking the packs she has.

There are...

5 packs of books, 10 books in each pack.

6 packs of pencils, 5 pencils in each pack.

8 packs of glue sticks, 2 glue sticks in each pack.

b) How many books are there altogether?

There are 50 books ~~all~~ altogether

8

Share

For each thing, first count how many groups, then how many in each group.

a) There are…

5 packs of books,
10 books in each pack.

6 packs of pencils,
5 pencils in each pack.

8 packs of glue sticks,
2 glue sticks in each pack.

	Number of packs	Number in each pack
	5	10
	6	5
	8	2

b)

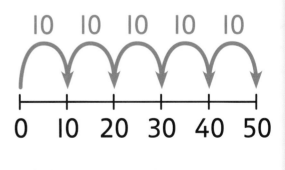

1	2	3	4	5	6	7	8	9	10
11	12	13	14	15	16	17	18	19	20
21	22	23	24	25	26	27	28	29	30
31	32	33	34	35	36	37	38	39	40
41	42	43	44	45	46	47	48	49	50

There are 50 books altogether.

Think together

1 How many pencils are there altogether?

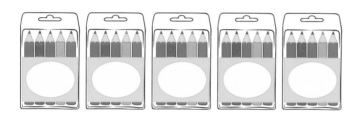

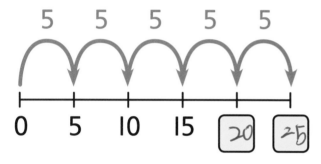

1	2	3	4	5	6	7	8	9	10
11	12	13	14	15	16	17	18	19	20
21	22	23	24	25	26	27	28	29	30
31	32	33	34	35	36	37	38	39	40
41	42	43	44	45	46	47	48	49	50

There are 25 pencils altogether.

2 How many glue sticks are there altogether?

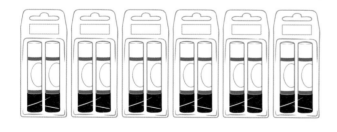

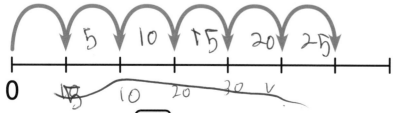

There are 25 glue sticks altogether.

10

3 8 packs of pens arrive.

CHALLENGE

There are 5 pens in each pack.

40

How many pens are there?

I will start by counting how many packs there are. How many pens are in each pack?

I wonder if I can count in groups to make it quicker to find out how many there are.

11

→ **Practice book 1C p6**

Making equal groups

Discover

1 a) How many  are there?

How many people are there in each  ?

b) How many  are there?

Are there the same number of people in each  ?

> I wonder which colour boats show **equal groups.**

Share

a)

2   2   2   2

There are 4 .

There are 2 people in each .

There are 4 groups of 2 people.

b)

1   3   5

There are 3  .

One  has 1 person in it.

One  has 3 people in it.

One  has 5 people in it.

The  show equal groups.

The  do not show equal groups.

13

Think together

1 How many glasses are there?

How many ice cubes are added to each glass?

There are ⑤ groups of ② ice cubes.

2 **a)** Look at the plates of cupcakes in A, B and C.

Which show equal groups?

Tell your friend why.

A   B   C

b) Look at the plates then complete this sentence.

There are ② equal groups of ④ cupcakes.

3 Which shows equal groups?

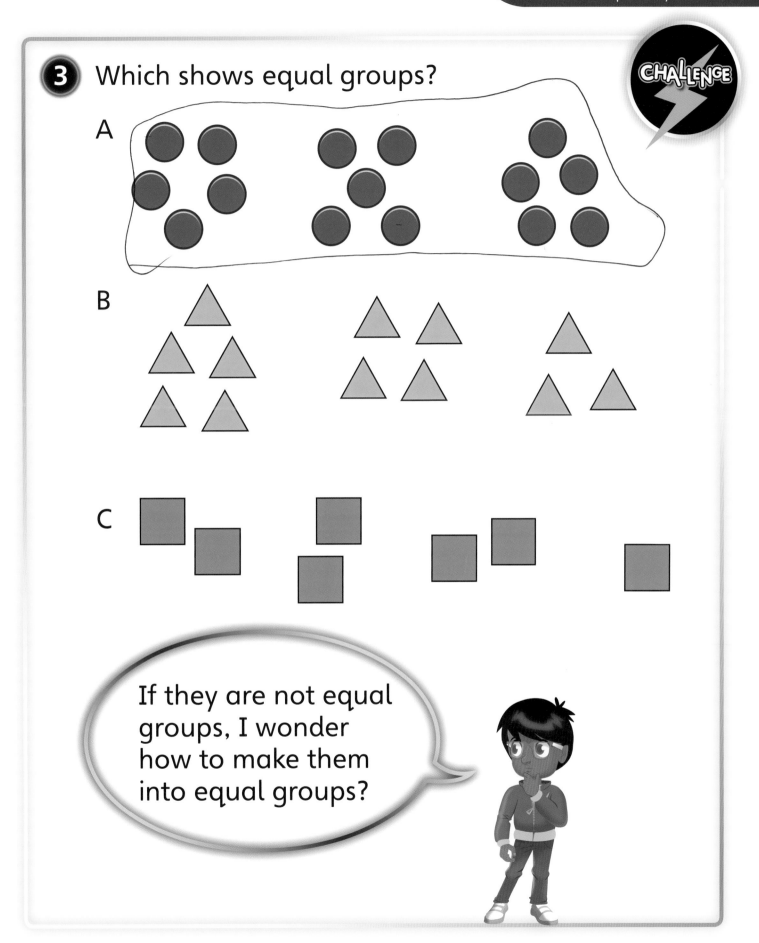

→ Practice book 1C p9

Adding equal groups

Discover

1 **a)** Millie bought 3 bunches of 🌼 .

How many 🌼 did she buy?

b) Dan bought 5 pairs of 👟 .

How many 👟 did he buy?

Share

a)

I used skip counting to help the addition.

I see this as an addition.

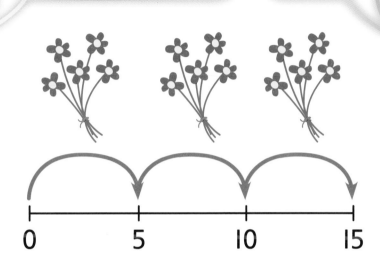

5 + 5 + 5 = 15

Millie bought 15 .

b)

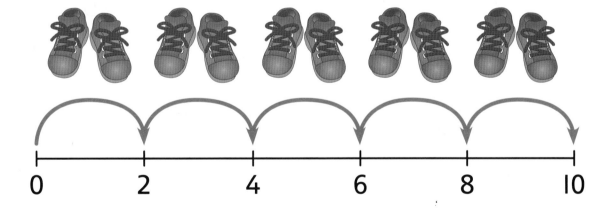

2 + 2 + 2 + 2 + 2 = 10

Dan bought 10 .

Think together

1 There are 7 bunches of  .

How many 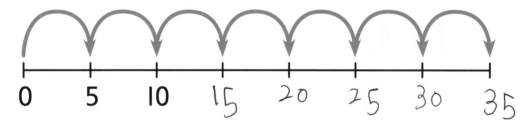 are there in total?

$5 + 5 + 5 + 5 + 5 + 5 + 5 = \boxed{35}$

There are $\boxed{35}$ 🌸 in total.

I can use skip counting to find the addition.

2 Dad bought 3 boxes of 10 eggs.

How many eggs did he buy?

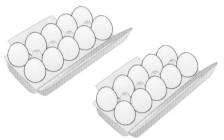  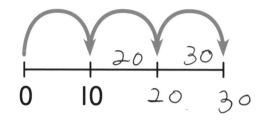

20   30

0   10   20   30

10 + 10 + 10 = 30   Dad bought 30 eggs.

3 Henry bought 3 packs of bread rolls.

 CHALLENGE

How many rolls did he buy?

4 + 4 + 4 = 12

I can try counting in 4s.

Let's try to find the answer by adding.

→ **Practice book 1C p12**

Making simple arrays

Discover

We have just planted some seeds.

1 **a)** How many seeds are there in each **row**? (10)

How many rows are there? (2)

How many seeds are there in total? (20)

b) Anya plants her seeds like this.

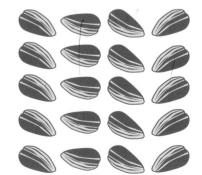

How many seeds are there in total?

20

✗ She has 20 seeds

Share

a)

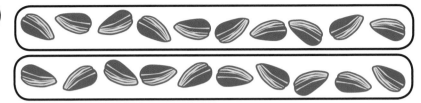

There are 10 seeds in each row.

There are 2 rows.

10 + 10 = 20

There are 20 seeds in total.

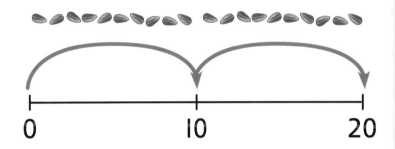

b)

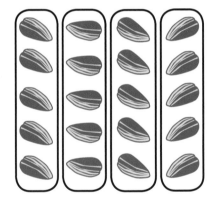

This arrangement is called an **array**.

There are 5 seeds in each **column**.

There are 4 columns.

5 + 5 + 5 + 5 = 20

There are 20 seeds in total.

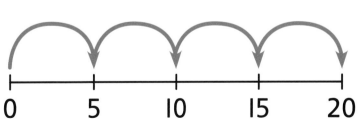

Think together

1 Complete the sentences for each array.

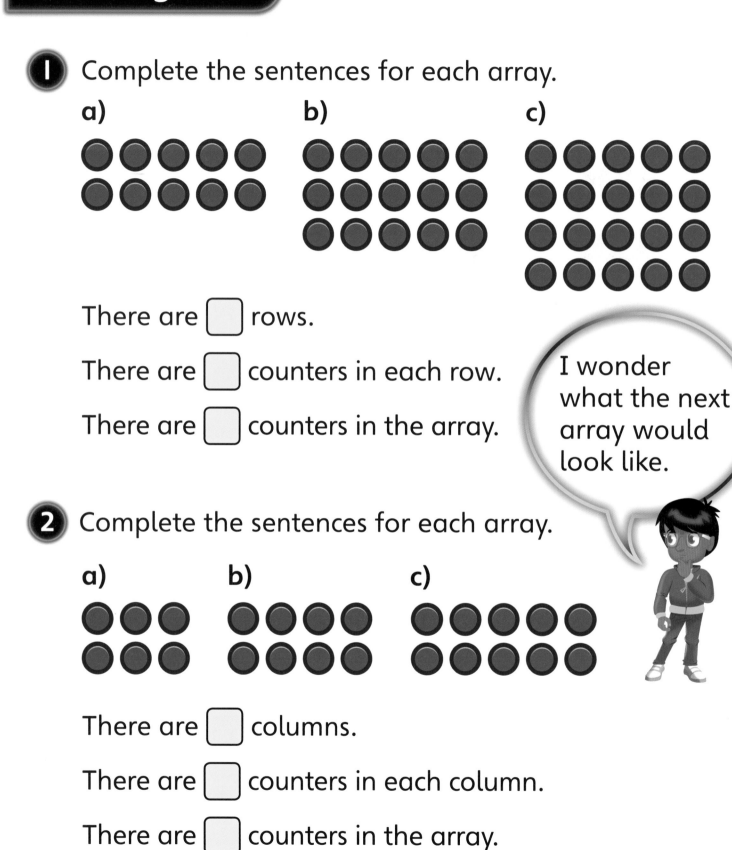

a)

b)

c)

There are ☐ rows.

There are ☐ counters in each row.

There are ☐ counters in the array.

I wonder what the next array would look like.

2 Complete the sentences for each array.

a)

b)

c)

There are ☐ columns.

There are ☐ counters in each column.

There are ☐ counters in the array.

3 How many chocolates are in each row and column?

How many chocolates are in each box?

a)

b)

c)

There are ☐ chocolates in a row.

There are ☐ chocolates in a column.

There are ☐ chocolates in the box.

I will count up using the rows.

I wonder whether I will get the same answer if I count up using the columns.

23

→ Practice book 1C p15

Making doubles

Discover

1 a) Who rolled a double?

What is double 4?

b) What is double 6?

Share

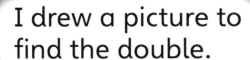

I drew a picture to find the double.

I added to find the double.

a) Tariq rolled a double.

Double 4 is two groups of 4.

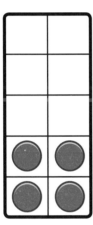 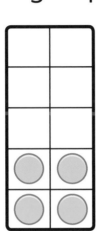 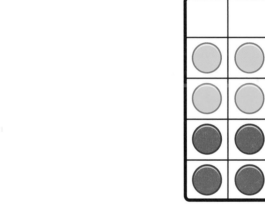

4   +   4   =   8   Double 4 is 8.

b) Double 6 is two groups of 6.

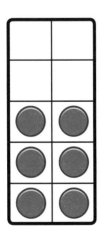 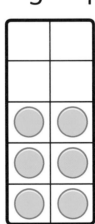 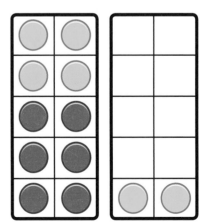

6   +   6   =   12   Double 6 is 12.

 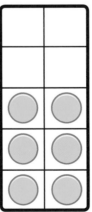

Think together

1 Complete the number sentences.

Number	Double	
		$1 + 1 = 2$
		$2 + 2 = \boxed{}$
		$3 + 3 = \boxed{}$
		$4 + \boxed{} = \boxed{}$
		$\boxed{} + \boxed{} = \boxed{}$
		$6 + 6 = 12$

2 What is double 8?

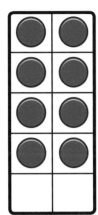 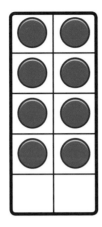

 +  =

Double 8 is ☐ .

I am going to learn my doubles.

3 Complete this table of doubles.

CHALLENGE

Number			3		5	6	7	8	9	10
Double	2	4		8						

27

→ Practice book 1C p18

Solving word problems – multiplication

Discover

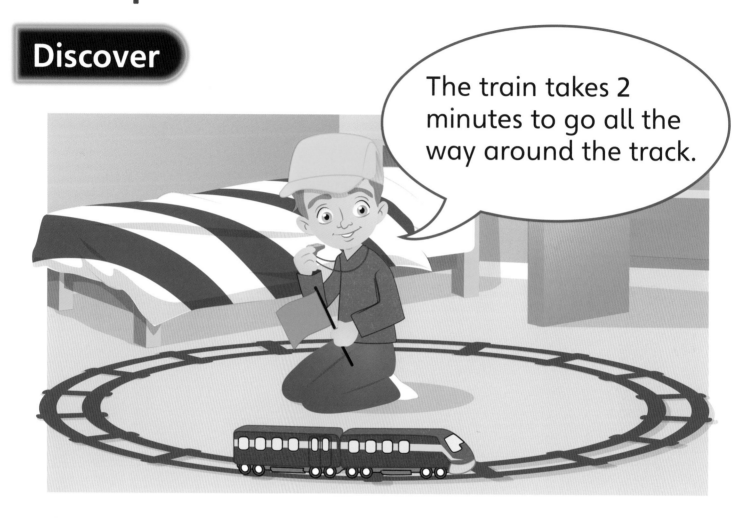

The train takes 2 minutes to go all the way around the track.

I **a)** How long does the train take to go around the track **twice**?

b) Charlie makes the track bigger.

The train now takes 5 minutes to go around the track. How long does it take to go around twice?

Twice means 2 times.

Share

a) Twice means 2 times.

  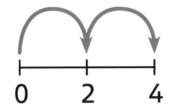

0   2   4

This reminds me of the doubles from last lesson.

$2 + 2 = 4$

The train takes 4 minutes to go around the track twice.

b)

$5 + 5 = 10$ Double 5 is 10.

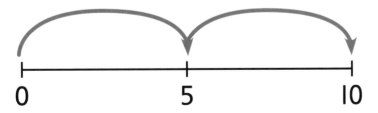

0   5   10

The train takes 10 minutes to go around the bigger track twice.

29

Think together

1 The car park is full.

There are 3 rows of 5 🚗.

How many 🚗 are in the car park?

> Draw the 🚗 to help you.
> Can you organise them in an array?

There are ☐ 🚗 in the car park.

2 An ice-cube tray has 2 rows of 8 holes.

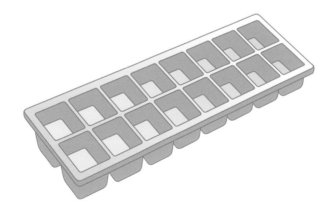

How many ice cubes are there in a full tray?

There are ☐ ice cubes in a full tray.

3 Who has more counters?

Izzy

Ben

_____ has more counters.

I counted in 5s and 10s.

I wonder if I could use doubles?

31

→ Practice book 1C p21

End of unit check

Your teacher will ask you these questions.

1 Which picture shows equal groups?

A

C

B

D

2 Which sentence describes the picture?

A 5 groups of 5 stars.   C 5 groups of 4 stars.

B 4 groups of 4 stars.   D 4 groups of 5 stars.

3 10 people can fit in each .

How many people can fit in these  in total?

A 10   B 4   C 40   D 14

4 Which array has 4 rows?

5 Which number completes both sentences?

8 is double ☐ .   Double 2 is ☐ .

A 4   B 8   C 1   D 2

Think!

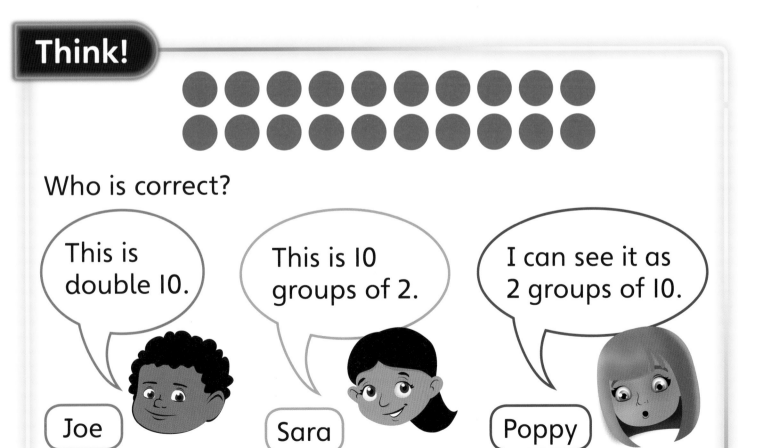

Who is correct?

This is double 10.

Joe

This is 10 groups of 2.

Sara

I can see it as 2 groups of 10.

Poppy

→ Practice book 1C p24

Unit 13
Division

In this unit we will …
- ⚡ Make equal groups
- ⚡ Share amounts equally
- ⚡ Solve word problems

Counters can help us show groups. Can you use counters to find how many groups of 2 flowers there are?

We will need some maths words. Which of these are new?

equal groups   **share**

We can also use a number line to help us. Can you put these into groups of 5? How many groups are there?

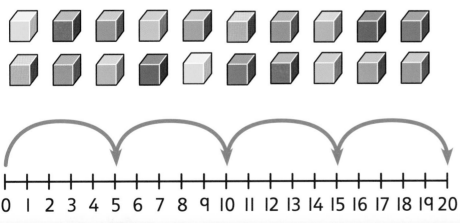

Making equal groups ❶

❶ **a)** 10 children stand in 3 groups.

Are the groups all equal?

b) The children now stand in groups of 2.

How many groups are there?

Share

I can show the groups using counters.

a) I group of 2

I group of 3

I group of 5

The groups have different numbers of children.

The children are not in equal groups.

b) There are 10 children altogether.

I will circle the children in groups of 2.

There are 2 children in each group.

There are 5 groups.

There are 5 groups of 2 children.

Think together

1 Here are 12 children.

They need to sit in groups of 4.

How many groups of children will there be?

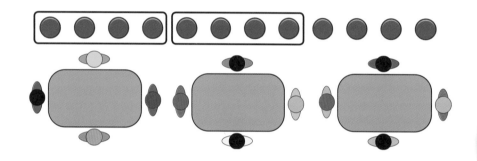

There are ☐ groups.

There are ☐ groups of ☐ children.

You can make an array to show the groups.

2 The 12 children are now put into groups of 3.

How many groups of children will there be?

There are ☐ groups.

There are ☐ children in each group.

There are ☐ groups of ☐ children.

3 Amy and Molly have 15 counters each.

I have put my counters into groups of 5.

I have put my counters into groups of 3.

Amy

Molly

Who has made the most groups?

I think it is Amy as she has the most in each group.

I am not sure if that is right. I will put them into groups to check.

39

→ Practice book 1C p26

Making equal groups ❷

Discover

❶ **a)** 5 balls fit into each box.

How many boxes are needed for 10 balls?

b) How many boxes are needed for 15 balls?

Share

a) There are 10 balls.

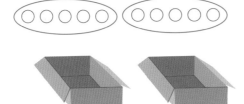

I will put all the balls into groups of 5. Then I will count how many groups there are.

2 boxes are needed for 10 balls.

5 balls in the first box, 5 balls in the second box.

I can use a

```
0 1 2 3 4 5 6 7 8 9 10 .
```

I start with 10 and subtract 5 each time.

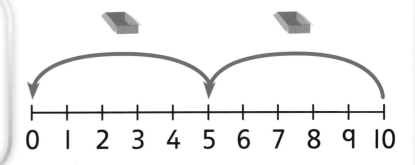

b) There are 5 balls in each box.

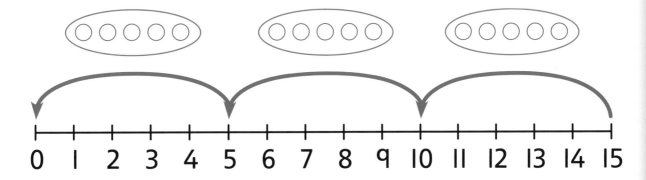

3 boxes are needed for 15 balls.

Think together

1 There are 30 balls.

5 balls fit into each box.

How many boxes are needed to fit all the balls?

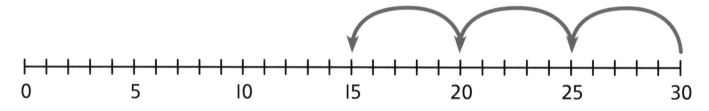

☐ boxes are needed to fit all the balls.

2

There are 12 bats. The bats are put into groups of 2.

How many groups are there?

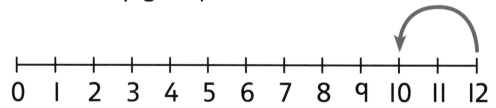

There are ☐ groups of ☐ bats.

3 Joe has some counters in a bag.

He puts the counters into groups.

He uses the number line to help him.

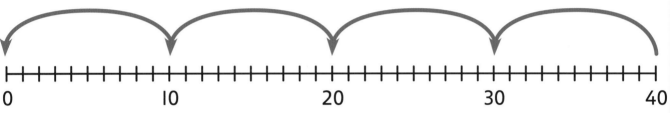

0   10   20   30   40

How many counters are in the bag?

How many counters are in each group?

How many groups are there?

Joe started at 40 and made 4 jumps of 10. I wonder if this will help me to work out the answers.

I am going to use ◯ to check.

43

→ **Practice book 1C p29**

Sharing equally ❶

Discover

❶ **a) Share** 8 ☁ between 4 pizzas.

How many ☁ should be on each pizza?

b) Share 12 🍅 on 4 pizzas.

How many 🍅 should be on each pizza?

Share

a) 8 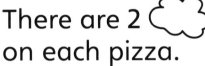 are shared between 4 pizzas.

Every pizza has the same amount of each topping. Share each topping out one at a time.

There are 2 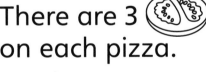 on each pizza.

Now there are 4 groups of 2.

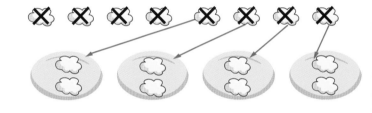

b) 12 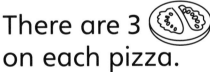 are shared between 4 pizzas.

There are 3 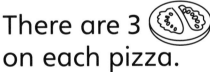 on each pizza.

Now there are 4 groups of 3.

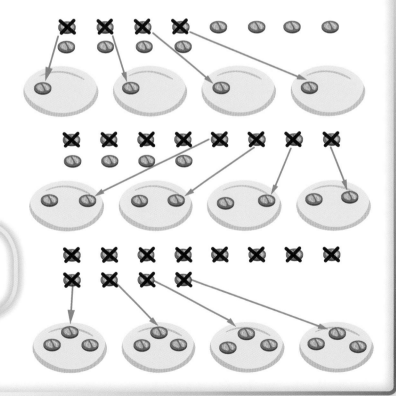

45

Think together

1 Share 16  between 4 pizzas.

How many should there be on each pizza?

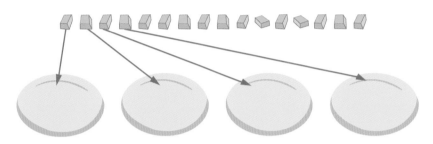

There are ☐ on each pizza.

Now there are ☐ groups of ☐.

2 Share 20 between 4 pizzas.

How many should there be on each pizza?

☐ are shared between ☐ pizzas.

There are ☐ on each pizza.

Now there are ☐ groups of ☐.

3 A pizza is cut into 12 slices.

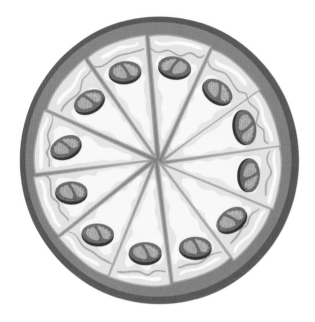

Sam and Mo share the slices equally.

How many slices do they each get?

I wonder what we are sharing between this time. Is it 4 again?

I don't think it is 4 again. We are sharing between 2 people. I will give them a slice each one by one.

47

Sharing equally ②

Discover

① **a)** Share the 12 ◯ equally between 4 children.

How many ◯ each?

b) Only 3 children play the next game.

The 12 ◯ are shared equally between them.

How many ◯ do they get each?

Share

I will give all the children I counter each until all the counters are used.

There is another way. I took a group of 4 counters and gave each person a counter.

a)

I each

2 each

3 each

There are 4 children.

Each child gets 3 counters.

There are 4 groups of 3 counters.

b)

There are 3 children playing the game.

Each child gets 4 counters.

There are 3 groups of 4 counters.

Think together

1 2 children are playing the game.

The 12 counters are shared equally between them.

How many counters do they get each?

They each get ☐ counters.

There are 2 groups of ☐ counters.

2 15 books are shared equally on 3 shelves.

How many books are there on each shelf?

There are ☐ books on each shelf.

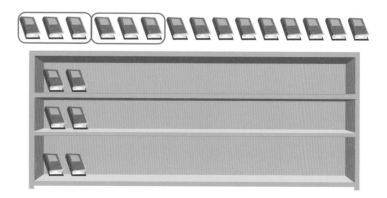

3 4 friends share 20 marbles equally.

CHALLENGE

How many marbles do they each get?

Write the matching statement.

Did you notice that everyone must get the same amount?

→ Practice book 1C p35

Solving word problems – division

Discover

Mrs Brown

1 **a)** There are 10 sheep.

The sheep are put in pens.

2 sheep go into each pen.

How many pens are needed?

b) Mrs Brown has 12 carrots.

She shares them equally between the 3 horses.

How many carrots does each horse get?

Share

I will put the sheep into groups of 2.

a)

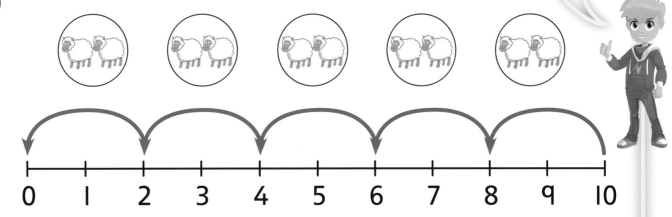

There are 5 groups of 2 sheep.

5 pens are needed for the sheep.

b)

I can share the carrots out equally between the 3 horses.

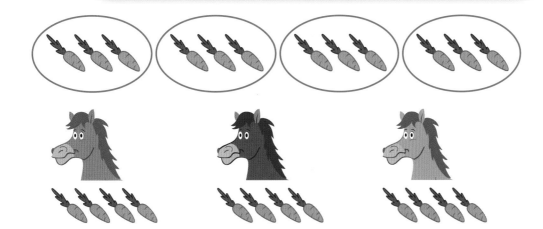

Each horse gets 4 carrots.

Think together

1 Mrs Brown's chickens lay 20 eggs in a day.

She puts 5 eggs into each box.

How many boxes does she need for 20 eggs?

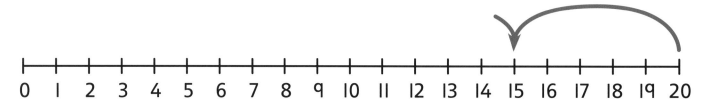

She needs ☐ boxes for 20 eggs.

2 Mr Brown makes 10 biscuits.

He shares them between 2 children.

How many biscuits will each child get?

Each child gets ☐ biscuits.

3 Mrs Brown needs 40 apples.

The apples come in
bags of 5 or bags of 10.

How many bags of 5 would she need?

How many bags of 10 would she need?

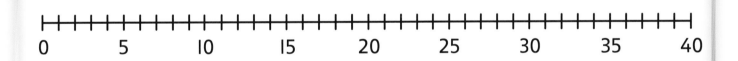

Mrs Brown needs ☐ bags with 5 apples in.

Mrs Brown needs ☐ bags with 10 apples in.

Would she need more bags
with 5 apples in, or more
bags with 10 apples in?

55

→ Practice book 1C p38

End of unit check

Your teacher will ask you these questions.

1 These 15 cubes are put in groups of 3.

How many equal groups will there be?

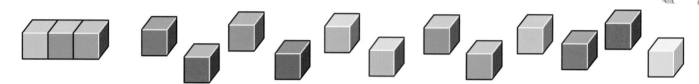

A 3 groups of 3

C 3 groups of 5

B 5 groups of 3

D 5 groups of 5

2 20 children are sorted into groups of 5.

Which number line shows how many equal groups of children there are?

A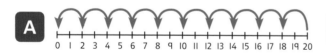

C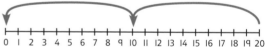

B

D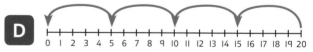

3 Jon has 3 fish tanks.
He shares 12 fish equally between the tanks.
How many fish will there be in each tank?

A 12   B 4   C 3   D 9

4 These 15 bean bags need to be sorted equally into the 3 buckets.

Which instruction is correct?

A Make groups of 3. **C** Make 3 groups.

B Put 10 in the first bucket. **D** Share them into 5 groups.

Think!

3 boys share 15 teddy bears equally.
2 girls share 12 teddy bears equally.

The boys say, 'We get more each because we have more in total.'

The girls say, 'We get more each because there are only 2 of us.'

Who is correct? Explain your answer.

Would your answer be the same if the boys had 18 teddy bears?

These words might help you.

share   equally   total

group   equal

→ Practice book 1C p41

Unit 14
Halves and quarters

In this unit we will ...
- ⚡ Find half of a shape or object
- ⚡ Share equally
- ⚡ Find a quarter of a shape or object
- ⚡ Solve word problems about halves and quarters

We can find half of a shape. Which shape has been cut in half?

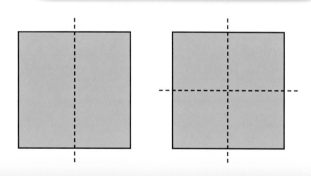

We will be using these maths words. Can you read them out loud?

half   **halves**   **quarter**

We will also do some sharing. Share the jam tarts equally. How many does each child get?

Finding halves ①

Discover

① **a)** How can the two gardeners share the flower bed equally?

b) Here are four squares.

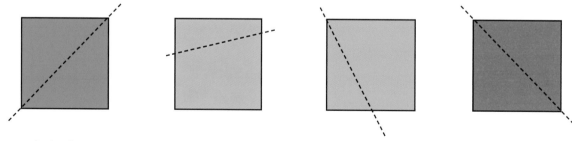

Which squares are split into **halves**?

Share

When you split a **whole** into two equal parts, each **part** is a **half**.

a) The flower bed is a square shape.

The gardeners can split the flower bed into two equal parts.

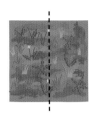 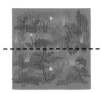

The two parts of the flower bed are equal, so it is split into two halves.

I wonder if **halves** always look the same.

I can check by folding or cutting a square piece of paper.

b) The two parts are not equal in these squares.

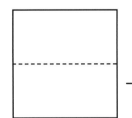

The two parts are equal in these squares. They are split into halves.

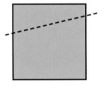

61

Think together

1 Here are six rectangles.

Which rectangles are split into two halves?

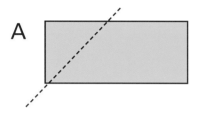
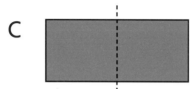
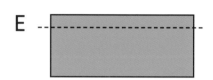

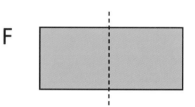

2 **a)** Which shapes are half shaded?

b) Which shapes are more than half shaded?

c) Which shapes are less than half shaded?

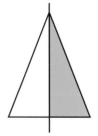

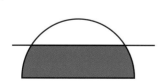
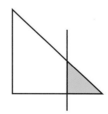
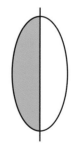

③

CHALLENGE

The gardeners have a piece of string.

How can they split the string into two halves?

Can you find
half of any line?

→ Practice book 1C p43

Finding halves ❷

Discover

Paul

Salma

1 **a)** Salma gives half of her apples to each horse.

How many apples does each horse get?

b) Paul has some apples in a bag.

He gives 2 apples to each donkey.

There are no more apples in the bag.

How many apples were in Paul's bag?

Share

a) There are 8 apples in Salma's bag.

I will share the whole bag of 8 apples into 2 equal parts.

Take 2 apples.

Give I apple to each horse.

Keep going until all the apples have been shared.

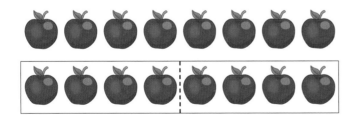

I can split the whole group into 2 equal parts.

4 apples is half of 8 apples.

Each horse gets 4 apples.

b) Paul gives 2 apples to each donkey.

Half of the apples in Paul's bag is 2.

2 apples is half of 4 apples.

There were 4 apples in Paul's bag.

Think together

You can use ◯ to help you share into 2 equal parts.

 Joe has 8 carrots.

He gives half of his carrots to each donkey.

How many carrots does each donkey get?

Half of 8 carrots is ☐ carrots.

Each donkey gets ☐ carrots.

2 Which groups of apples have been shared into halves?

A 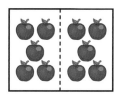 B 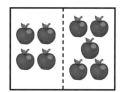 C 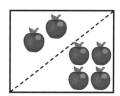 D

3 Complete the sentences.

CHALLENGE

a)

Half of 10 apples is ☐ apples.

b)

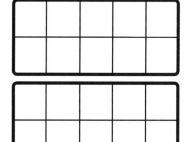

Half of ☐ _____ is ☐ _____.

c)

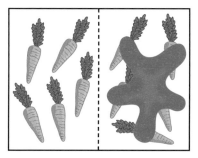

Half of ☐ carrots is 5 carrots.

→ Practice book 1C p46

Finding quarters ❶

Discover

You have to land on red. I have to land on yellow.

❶ **a)** Are these boards split into equal parts?

b) Are any of these boards split into **quarters**?

 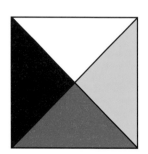 

Share

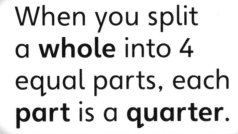

When you split a **whole** into 4 equal parts, each **part** is a **quarter**.

The boards look different. I think they are both split into quarters.

a) Both boards are split into 4 equal parts.

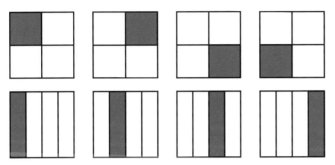

They are both split into quarters.

b) This board is not split into quarters.

The parts are not equal.

These boards are split into 4 equal parts.

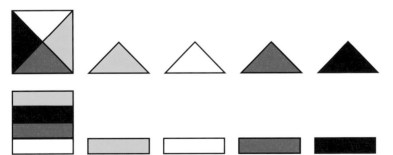

These boards are split into quarters.

Think together

1 Which of these boards are split into quarters?

A   B   C   D

2 Which of these shapes are split into quarters?

A

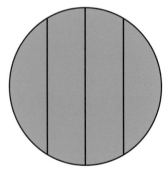

C

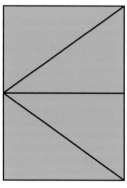

B

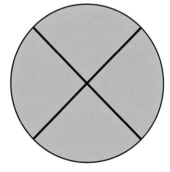

D

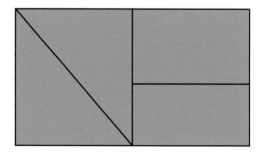

70

3 This is a quarter of a shape.

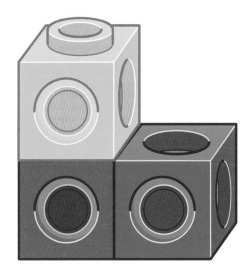

What could the whole shape be?

Four quarters
make one whole.

I am going to
use  to make
the shape.

71

Finding quarters ②

Discover

l **a)** The children share the oranges equally.

How many does each child get?

b) This is a quarter.

What is the whole?

Share

a) There are 8 oranges.

> I wonder if we can share them equally between 4 people.

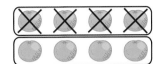
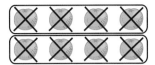

> To share between 4 I can split them into quarters.

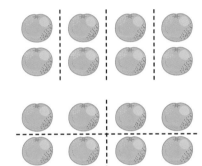

Each child gets 2 oranges.

b)

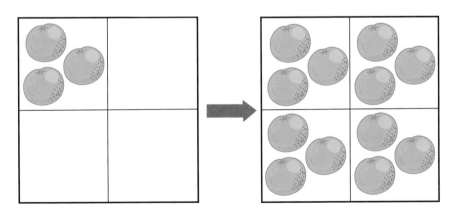

There are 3 oranges in each quarter.

The whole is 12 oranges.

Think together

1. Split these into quarters.

    a) 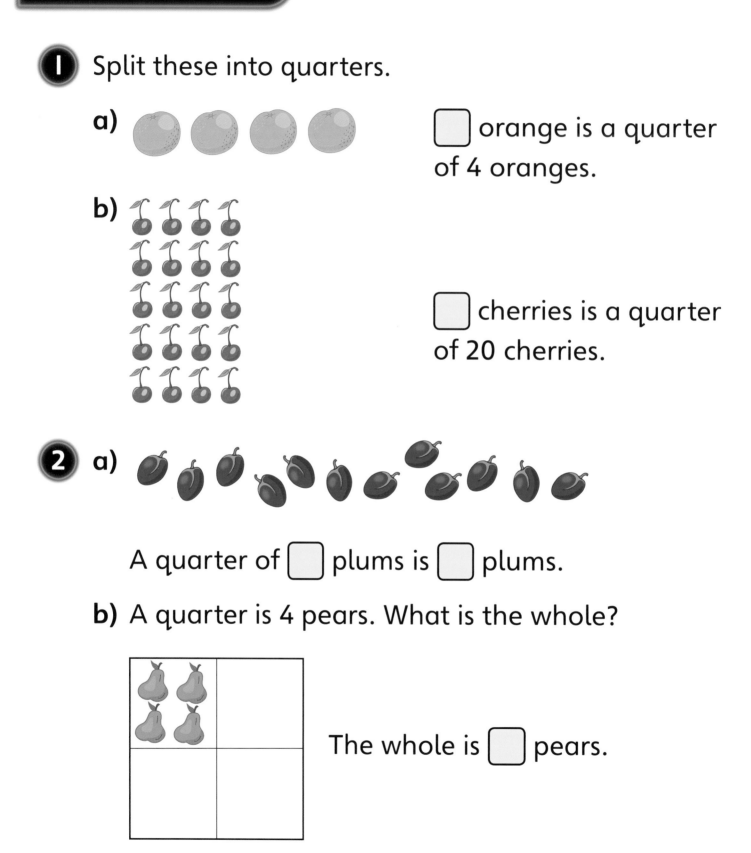 ☐ orange is a quarter of 4 oranges.

    b) ☐ cherries is a quarter of 20 cherries.

2. a) A quarter of ☐ plums is ☐ plums.

    b) A quarter is 4 pears. What is the whole?

    The whole is ☐ pears.

3 Which of these are a quarter full?

Which are more than a quarter full?

CHALLENGE

a)

b)

c)

I wonder how many quarters make a whole.

d)

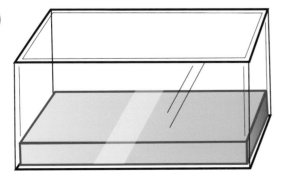

75

Solving word problems – halves and quarters

Discover

1 **a)** A quarter of the people are vegetarians.

How many people are vegetarians?

b) Which drink is half full?

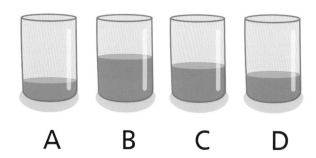

Share

a)

It says a quarter. I'll find out how many people that is.

I think a quarter is the part compared to the whole.

The whole is 8 people.

Split the whole into quarters.

Find one of the quarters.

I could also arrange it like this.

A quarter of 8 people is 2 people.

2 people are vegetarians.

b) 2 halves fill the whole glass.

Glass B is half full.

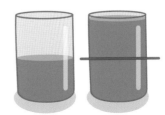

Think together

1 How many will he eat?

I can only eat half of my potatoes.

Tom

Half of ☐ 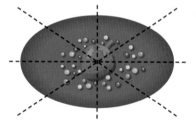 is ☐  .

2 Dad cuts these cakes.

A

C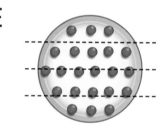

E

B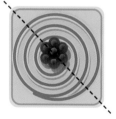

D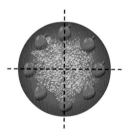

F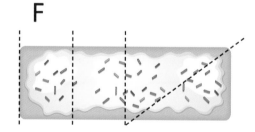

Which cake is cut into halves?

Cake _____ is cut into halves.

Which cake is cut into quarters?

Cake _____ is cut into quarters.

3 **a)** How many rolls were there on the whole plate?

CHALLENGE

You have already eaten half of the rolls.

I wonder how many halves make a whole.

There were ☐ rolls on the plate.

b) How many candles were on the whole cake?

I can work out how many quarters make a whole.

A quarter of the candles are on my cake.

There were ☐ candles on the cake.

79

→ Practice book 1C p55

End of unit check

Your teacher will ask you these questions.

1 Which pizza is cut into halves?

A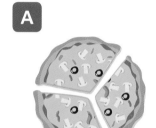

B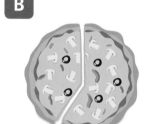

C

D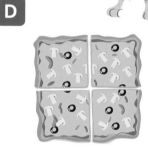

2 There are 12 frogs. Half are male.

How many are male?

A 10   **B** 6   **C** 2   **D** 12

3 Which window is not split into quarters?

A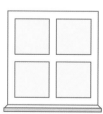

B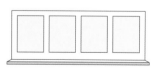

C

D

4 Which number completes both sentences?

2 is half of ☐.

☐ is a quarter of 16.

A 1   **B** 8   **C** 4   **D** 2

Think!

Luke says, 'I would like half of them.'

Eva says, 'I would like a quarter, please.'

Luke works out half, but Eva is stuck.

Can you explain why?

These words might help you.

half   quarter

whole   part

split

→ Practice book 1C p58

Unit 15
Position and direction

In this unit we will …
- ⚡ Describe turns
- ⚡ Use the words left and right
- ⚡ Say if something is at the top, middle or bottom

We will use these arrows to show turns. Which one do you think shows a whole turn?

  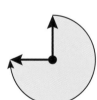 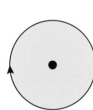

These maths words help us talk about where something is. Do you know any of these?

turn   half turn   quarter turn

three-quarter turn   whole turn   position

left   right   forwards   backwards

above   below   top   middle   bottom

up   down   in between

Look at where these animals are. Which animal is on the bottom shelf?

83

Describing turns

Discover

1 **a)** David makes a **half turn**.

What is he facing?

b) David is facing the .

He moves to face the .

What **turn** could he have made?

Share

a)

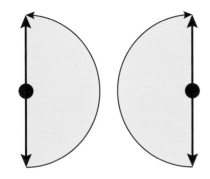

These are half turns.

David is facing the .

> For a half turn, it is the same no matter which way you turn.

b)

> I think David has made a quarter turn.

 This is a **quarter turn**.

These are quarter turns too.

> I think he has made a three-quarter turn.

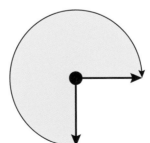

This is a **three-quarter turn**.

David could have made a quarter turn or a three-quarter turn.

85

Think together

1 David is facing the .

He makes a half turn.

What is he facing?

2 The makes a quarter turn.

Which image in the box below shows the new **position** of the ?

A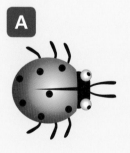

B

C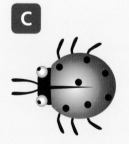

D

86

3

CHALLENGE

Laura is facing the .

She makes a half turn.

She is facing the .

Which box is the in?

What happens if Laura makes a **whole turn**? Where is she facing?

87

→ Practice book 1C p60

Describing positions ❶

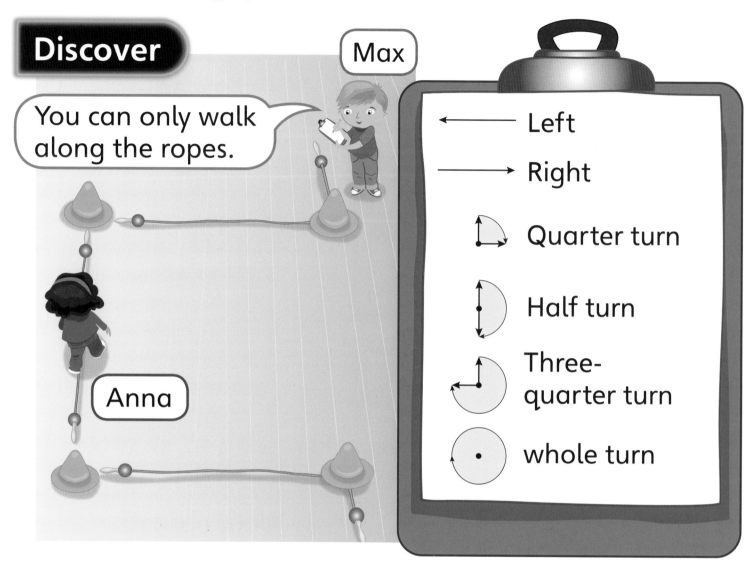

Discover

Max

You can only walk along the ropes.

Anna

→ Left

→ Right

Quarter turn

Half turn

Three-quarter turn

whole turn

❶ **a)** When Anna gets to the next 🔺, what turn will she make?

Will she turn **left** or **right**?

b) What does Max need to say to Anna to help her get to the end of the maze?

Share

This is a right turn.

This is a left turn.

a) Anna will make a quarter turn right.

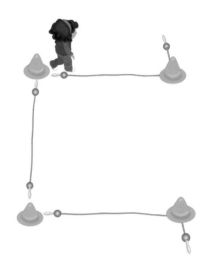

Anna will turn right.

b) Walk **forwards**. Make a quarter turn left. Walk forwards.

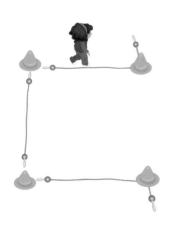

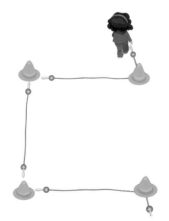

Think together

1 Describe Anna's route. Put the sentences in the correct order using 1, 2 and 3.

Walk 3 steps forwards. ☐

Make a quarter turn left. ☐

Walk 4 steps forwards. ☐

Finish

Start

2 Complete the sentences to describe Anna's route.

Finish   Start

First walk ☐ steps _____ .

Then make a _____ turn _____ .

Next walk ☐ steps _____ .

After that make a _____ turn _____ .

Finally walk ☐ steps _____ .

forwards   left   right
quarter turn   half turn   three-quarter turn

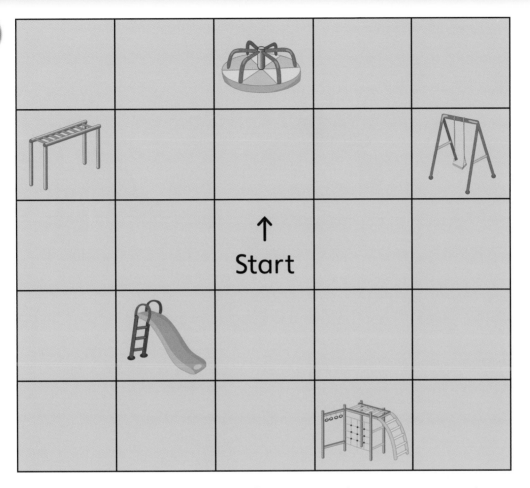

Begin at Start and follow the instructions.

Where do you end up?

1   Walk I square forwards.

2   Make a quarter turn left.

3   Walk 2 squares forwards.

Can you make up your own story to get to a different place in the playground?

→ Practice book 1C p63

Describing positions ❷

Discover

1 a) What is **above** the ?

b) Describe the position of the 🐻 .

Share

a)

The are above the .

What is the on top of?

b)

top

middle

bottom

The is on the bottom shelf.

The is **below** the  .

I described the position in a different way!

The teddy is to the right of the .

Think together

1 Look at the  .

Which shelf are they on?

The are on the _____ shelf.

2 Complete the sentences.

The is going _____ the slide.

The is climbing _____ the rope.

up   down   **bottom**   **middle**   **top**

3 Describe the position of the .

The  is on the top shelf.

The  is to the right of the 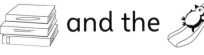 .

Are the two children correct?

Are there other ways you can describe the position of the doll?

I can write a sentence using **in between**. The  is in between the  and the  .

95

→ **Practice book 1C p66**

End of unit check

Your teacher will ask you these questions.

1 Which sentence **does not** describe the image?

A The  is to the left of the  .

B The  is in between the and the .

C The  is to the right of the .

D The 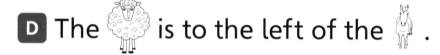 is to the left of the .

2 Complete the sentence.

The is _____ the .

A above   **C** to the right of

B below   **D** to the left of

3 David is facing the .

He turns a quarter turn left.

What is he facing now?

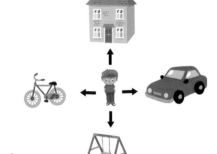

A B  C  D

4 David is facing the .

He turns so he is facing the .

Describe the turn.

David made a _____ turn.

A quarter   B half   C three-quarter   D whole

Think!

Can you guide the mouse to the cheese?

Can you find more than one path?

These words might help you.

forwards   backwards

square   left   right

half turn   quarter turn

three-quarter turn

→ Practice book 1C p69

Unit 16
Numbers to 100

In this unit we will …
- ⚡ Count in tens
- ⚡ Learn how to use a 100 square
- ⚡ Use tens and ones to make larger numbers
- ⚡ Say which number is larger and smaller
- ⚡ Find numbers which add to 100

We will use this 100 square. Can you find number 30?

1	2	3	4	5	6	7	8	9	10
11	12	13	14	15	16	17	18	19	20
21	22	23	24	25	26	27	28	29	30
31	32	33	34	35	36	37	38	39	40
41	42	43	44	45	46	47	48	49	50
51	52	53	54	55	56	57	58	59	60
61	62	63	64	65	66	67	68	69	70
71	72	73	74	75	76	77	78	79	80
81	82	83	84	85	86	87	88	89	90
91	92	93	94	95	96	97	98	99	100

We will need some maths words. Can you read these out loud?

100 square   **number square**

place value grid

We will need this too. What number is shown here?

Tens	Ones

Counting to 100

Discover

1 a) Count out 52 counters.

How did you count them?

b) How many more pieces of litter does Gaby need to collect before she goes to the park manager again?

Share

I ◯ represents
I piece of litter.

a)

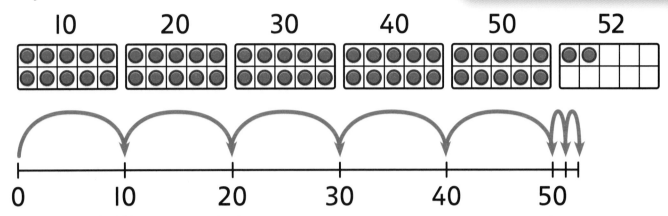

I kept losing count when I counted them one by one.

I put them into tens first. This made it easier to count. I then counted in tens.

b) Gaby needs to have 10 pieces of litter to take to the park manager.

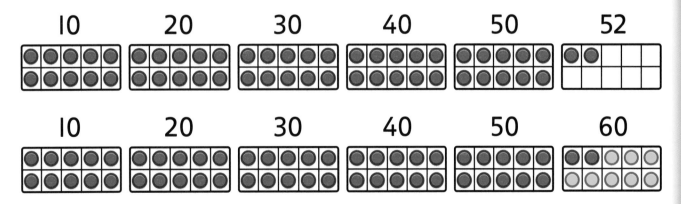

Gaby needs to collect 8 more pieces of litter.

Think together

I How many are there?

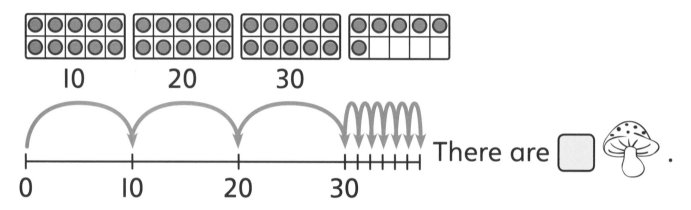

There are ☐ .

It's difficult to fit all these jumps on the number line.

I think I could count the ones all in one go.

2 How many are there?

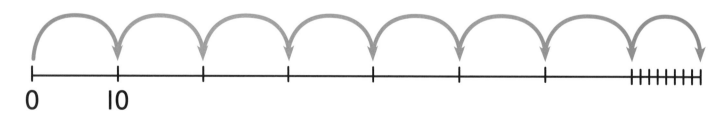

There are ☐ .

3 Find the mistakes.

a)

There are 67 sweets in total.

b)

| 50 | 51 | 53 | 54 | 55 | 56 | 57 | 58 |

c)

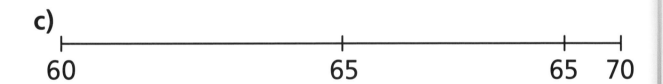

60   65   65   70

I think there is a number missing from the number track.

I think there is a mistake in each one.

103

Exploring number patterns

Discover

1 **a)** What number do the children need to put next?

b) Where does the **36** go on the **100 square**?

Share

a)

I counted on from 26.
The number after 26 is 27.

1	2	3	4	5	6	7	8	9	10
11	12	13	14	15	16	17	18	19	20
21	22	23	24	25	26	27	28	29	30

b)

I saw a pattern. All the numbers that end in 6 are in the same column.

The pattern shows us that 36 will go below 26.

1	2	3	4	5	6	7	8	9	10
11	12	13	14	15	16	17	18	19	20
21	22	23	24	25	26	27	28	29	30
31	32	33	34	35	36	37	38	39	40
41	42	43	44	45	46	47	48	49	50
51	52	53	54	55	56	57	58	59	60
61	62	63	64	65	66	67	68	69	70
71	72	73	74	75	76	77	78	79	80
81	82	83	84	85	86	87	88	89	90
91	92	93	94	95	96	97	98	99	100

Each column goes up or down in tens.

105

Think together

1

									20
21	22	23	24	25	26	27	28	29	30
31	32	33	34	35	36	37	38	39	40
41	42	43	44	45	46	47	48	49	50

What is I more than 43?

What is I less than 43?

> Where are these on the **number square**?

One more than 43 is ☐.

One less than 43 is ☐.

2 What numbers are covered in the number square?

41	42	43	44	🟤	46	47	48	49	50
51	52	53	54	55	🟤				
61	62	63	64	🟤	66	67	68	69	70
			74	🟤				🟤	

Numbers ☐, ☐, ☐, ☐ and ☐ are covered.

3 Copy the diagram and fill in the boxes.

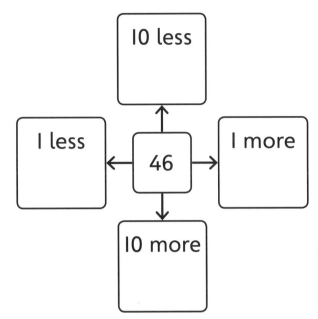

Where are these numbers on the 100 square?

1	2	3	4	5	6	7	8	9	10
11	12	13	14	15	16	17	18	19	20
21	22	23	24	25	26	27	28	29	30
31	32	33	34	35	36	37	38	39	40
41	42	43	44	45	46	47	48	49	50
51	52	53	54	55	56	57	58	59	60
61	62	63	64	65	66	67	68	69	70
71	72	73	74	75	76	77	78	79	80
81	82	83	84	85	86	87	88	89	90
91	92	93	94	95	96	97	98	99	100

I think one more is always the next number.

How can I use the 100 square to count up in tens from 8?

107

→ Practice book 1C p74

Partitioning numbers ❶

Discover

❶ **a)** How many days of ☀ have there been?

b) How many full rows of 10 are there?

How many more ☀ are there?

Share

a)

I counted one at a time.

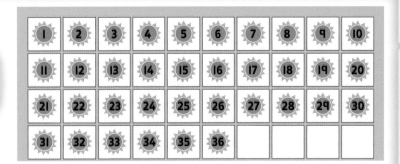

There are 10 in each row. I counted in tens and then added the ones.

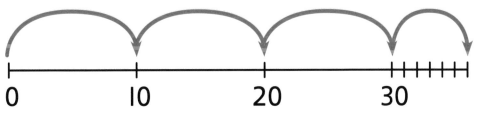

There have been 36 days of .

b)

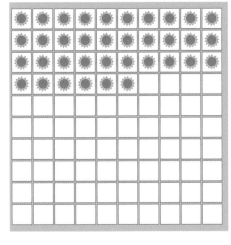

I will use a **place value grid**.

There are 3 full rows of 10.

There are 6 more .

Tens	Ones
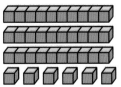	
3	6

109

Think together

  1

	Days of 💧								
💧	💧	💧	💧	💧	💧	💧	💧	💧	💧
💧	💧	💧	💧	💧	💧	💧	💧	💧	💧
💧	💧	💧	💧	💧	💧	💧	💧	💧	💧
💧	💧	💧	💧	💧	💧	💧	💧	💧	💧
💧	💧	💧	💧	💧	💧	💧	💧	💧	💧
💧	💧	💧	💧	💧	💧	💧	💧	💧	💧
💧	💧								

How many days of ⬡ have there been?

There are ☐ rows of 10.

There are ☐ more.

There have been ☐ days of ⬡ .

2 What numbers are shown each time?

a)

Tens	Ones

c)

Tens	Ones

b)

Tens	Ones

d)

Tens	Ones

3 Gaby makes a number.

What number has Gaby made?

I think I can exchange ten for something to make this easier.

I will put Gaby's number into a place value grid.

III

→ Practice book 1C p77

Partitioning numbers ❷

Discover

1 **a)** There are 10 chairs in each stack.

How many chairs are there in total?

b) Show the number of chairs in total on a place value grid.

Share

a)

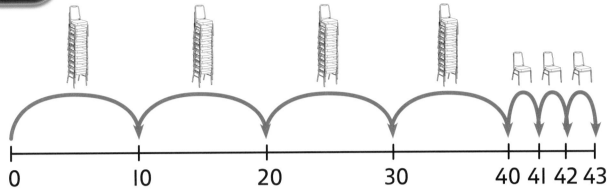

There are 4 stacks of 10 chairs.

There are 3 more chairs.

There are 43 chairs in total.

I didn't have to count the chairs in each stack.
I know there are 10 chairs in each stack.
I counted in tens first and then in ones.

b)

Tens	Ones
4	3

Tens	Ones
4	3

4 tens and 3 ones = 43

43 = 40 + 3

Think together

1

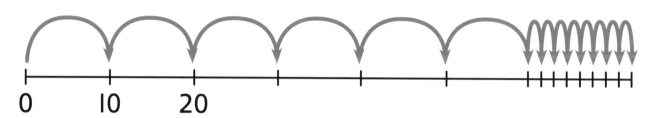

0   10   20

How many chairs are there in total?

There are ☐ stacks of 10 chairs.

There are ☐ extra chairs.

There are ☐ chairs in total.

Is there a better way to add the 1s?

2 What numbers are shown each time?

a)

Tens	Ones
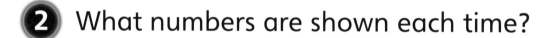	◇ ◇

☐ tens and ☐ ones = ☐

☐ = 50 + 2

b)

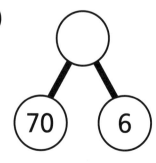

70   6

c)

CHALLENGE

3 Put all the 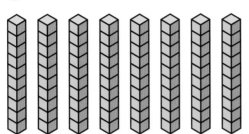 on the place value grids to make two numbers.

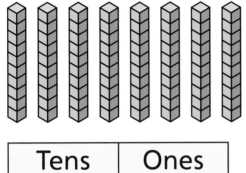

Tens	Ones

Tens	Ones

What numbers did you make?

One of my numbers is 26. I wonder what the other number will be?

115

Comparing numbers ❶

Discover

❶ **a)** Use 🔲 to show the number of 🐚 each

child has.

b) Who has the most 🐚, Ray or Tamsin?

Share

a)

Ray

 35

Tamsin  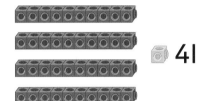 4l

One  shows 10 🐚 .

A 🎲 shows 1 🐚 .

b) Ray

 35

Tamsin

41

35 < 4l

Tamsin has the most 🐚 .

Think together

1 Who has fewer flags, Ray or Tamsin?

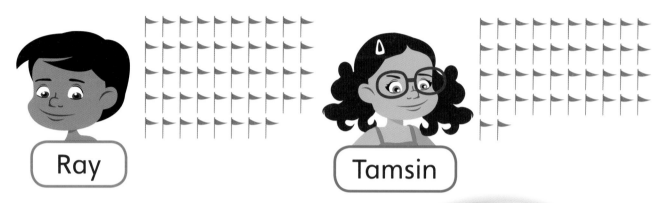

Ray

Tamsin

_____ has fewer flags.

I used 🎲 to compare the flags.

2 Use <, > or = to complete a number sentence for each diagram.

a)

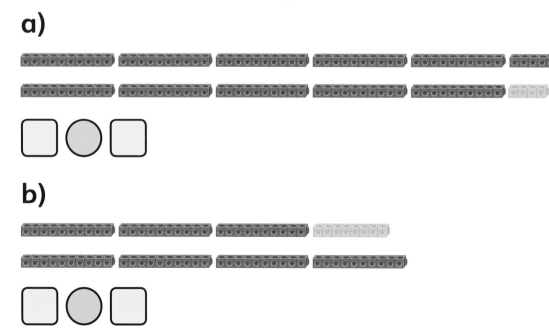

b)

3 Which number is greater?

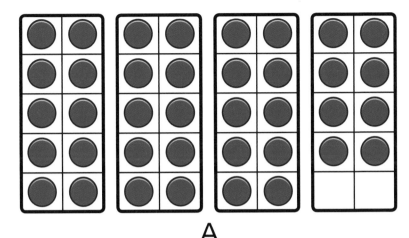

A

B

[ ] is greater than [ ].

I compared them using .

I compared them using a .

Comparing numbers ②

Discover

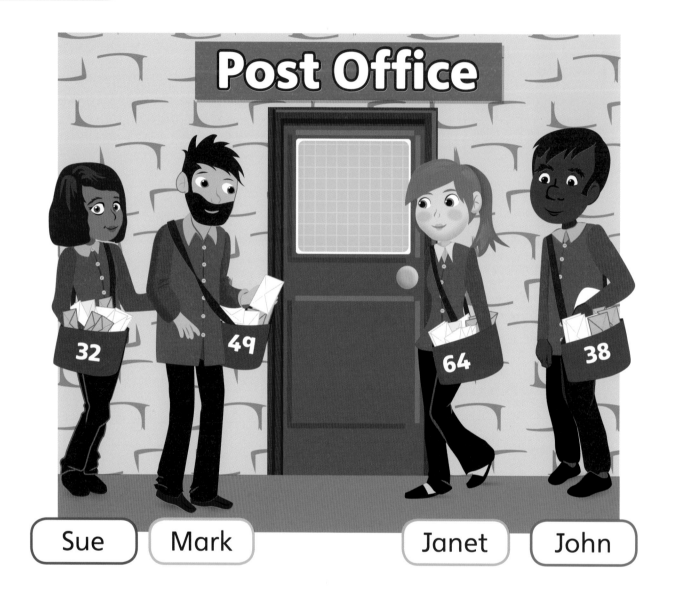

Sue   Mark   Janet   John

1   **a)** Who has the most ✉ to deliver, Mark or Janet?

     b) Who has the most ✉ to deliver, John or Sue?

Share

a)

Janet

Mark

Tens	Ones

Tens	Ones

I lined them up so I could see who has the most letters.

   64

                                    49

64 is greater than 49.

64 > 49

Janet has 6 tens.

Mark has 4 tens.

I didn't line them up.
I just compared the tens.

Janet has the most ✉ to deliver.

b)

Sue

John

Tens	Ones

Tens	Ones

I compared the tens first. They had the same number of tens.

Tens	Ones

Tens	Ones

As they had the same number of tens, I compared the ones next. John had more ones.

32 is less than 38.

32 < 38

John has the most ✉ to deliver.

Think together

1 Choose <, > or = to complete the sentences.

38 ◯ 31   31 ◯ 26   26 ◯ 38

2 Look at the number cards. Use the cards to make a 2-digit number to go in each circle.

CHALLENGE

4 5 6 7

| Greater than 60 | Between 58 and 68 | In the sequence that starts 0, 5, 10, 15, 20 … |

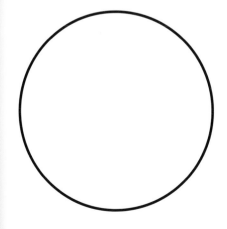 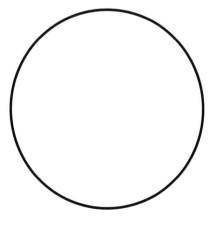 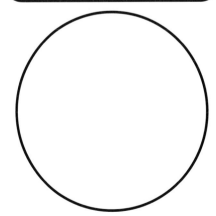

123

Ordering numbers

Discover

1 **a)** Order the number of 🥄 of porridge from smallest to greatest.

   b) Which bowl belongs to which child?

Share

I made each number out of  and lined them up.

a)

Alisha

Maya

Eshan

25 is the smallest.

27 is the next smallest.

45 is the greatest.

25 < 27 < 45

I put each number into a place value grid and compared the tens. Then I compared the ones.

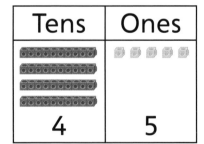

Tens	Ones		Tens	Ones		Tens	Ones
4	5		2	5		2	7

45 has the most tens so this is the greatest.

25 and 27 have the same number of tens.

25 has fewer ones than 27.

25 is the smallest number.

25 < 27 < 45

b)

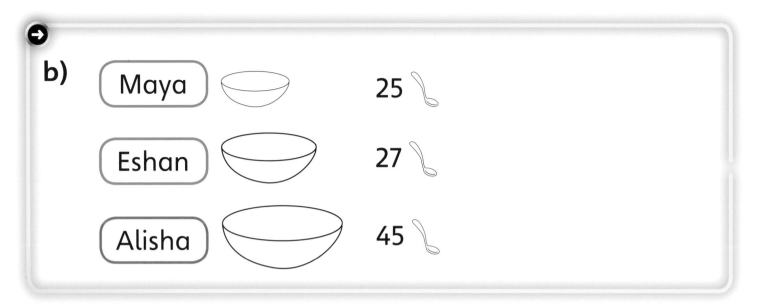

Maya   25

Eshan   27

Alisha   45

Think together

1

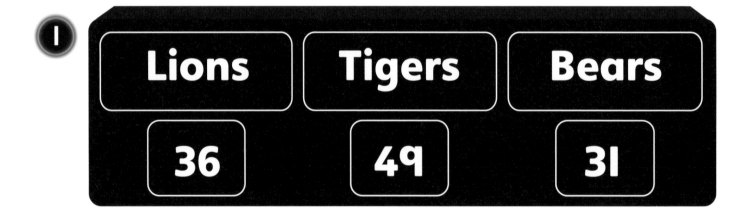

Lions	Tigers	Bears
36	49	31

Put the scores in order from fewest to most points.

Lions
Tigers
Bears

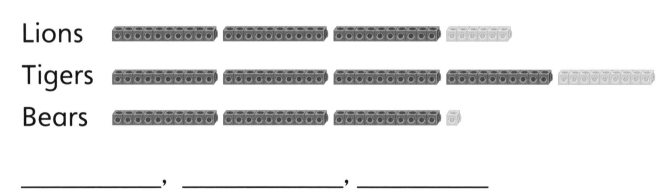

_____, _____, _____

Fewest points   Most points

2 Here are three numbers.

Tens	Ones

Tens	Ones

Tens	Ones

Put the numbers in order from greatest to smallest.

☐ > ☐ > ☐

3 Ali and Jill make 2-digit numbers with the number cards below.

| 1 | 3 | 7 | 8 |

What numbers could they make?

127

Bonds to 100 ①

Discover

① **a)** How many counters does Cora have?

How many ⚪ ?

How many ⚫ ?

b) Draw a diagram to show this.

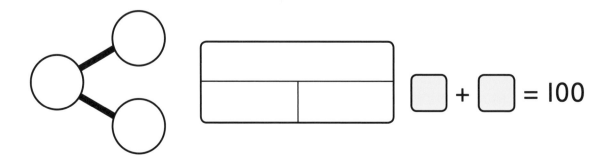

$\square + \square = 100$

Share

a)

> I remembered to count in tens so it was quicker.

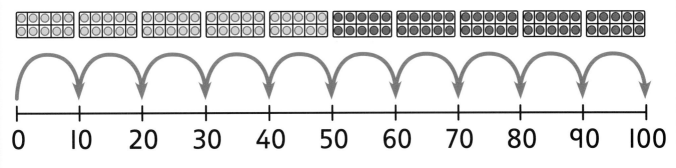

There are 100 counters.

There are 50 .

There are 50 .

b)

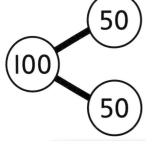

100	
50	50

$50 + 50 = 100$

> 50 is a part. 50 is a part. 100 is the whole. These make a number bond to 100.

> I remember number bonds to 10. $5 + 5 = 10$. I think I can see a connection.

Think together

1 Cora changes 10 red counters to 10 yellow counters.

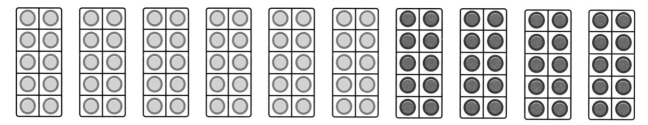

Write a new bond to 100.

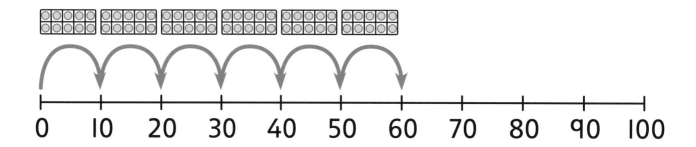

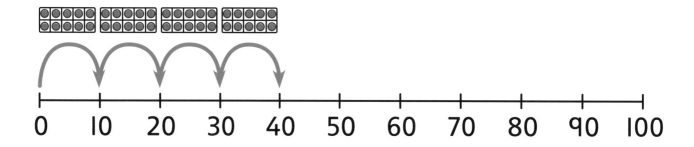

☐ + ☐ = 100

2 Cora uses the string to make bonds to 100.

Complete the bonds to 100.

a) ☐ + ☐ = 100

b) ☐ + ☐ = 100

3 Use ▢▢▢▢▢ or string to try and find all of

the ten bonds that make 100.

CHALLENGE

☐ + ☐ = 100   ☐ + ☐ = 100

☐ + ☐ = 100   ☐ + ☐ = 100

☐ + ☐ = 100   ☐ + ☐ = 100

☐ + ☐ = 100   ☐ + ☐ = 100

☐ + ☐ = 100   ☐ + ☐ = 100

How can I make sure I do not miss any bonds?

I wonder if some of these bonds are the same.

131

→ Practice book 1C p92

Bonds to 100 2

Discover

Eddie

1 **a)** How many different stamps has Eddie used?

How many stamps has Eddie not used?

☐ + ☐ = 10

b) How many squares on the wall have stamps in them?

How many squares do not have stamps in them?

☐ + ☐ = 100

Share

a) Eddie has 10 stamps.

Eddie has used 3 of the stamps.

Eddie has not used 7 of the stamps.

$3 + 7 = 10$

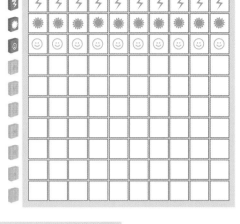

b)

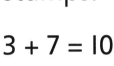

Each row has 10 squares in it. I counted in tens.

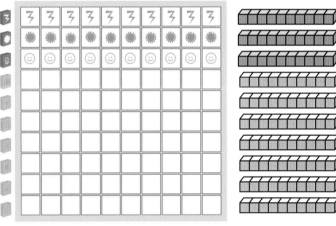

There are 100 squares on the grid.

30 squares have stamps in them.

70 squares do not have stamps in them.

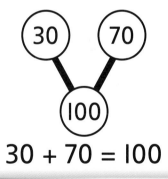

$30 + 70 = 100$

If I know that $3 + 7 = 10$ then I can work out that $30 + 70 = 100$.

Can you see how the first answer helps you with the second answer?

Think together

1 Complete each sentence.

There are 10 stamps.

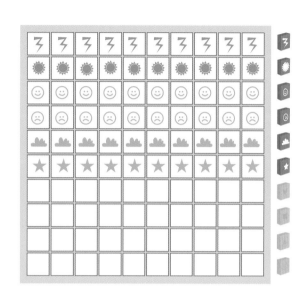

☐ stamps are used.

☐ stamps are not used.

☐ + ☐ = 10

There are 100 squares.

☐ squares have stamps in them.

☐ squares do not have stamps in them.

☐ + ☐ = 100

2 Complete the number facts.

1 + 9 = ☐

10 + ☐ = 100

☐ + 20 = 100

☐ + 2 = 10

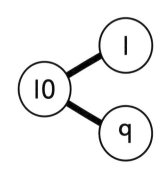

100	
80	20

3

Each on my ☐☐☐☐☐ represents 10.

CHALLENGE

What bond does the  show?

☐ + ☐ = ☐

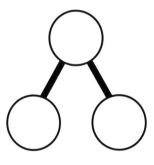

I think it might show something different.

I wonder what other bonds I can show.

That is easy. It shows 6 + 4 = 10.

135

End of unit check

Your teacher will ask you these questions.

1 How many biscuits are there?

| A 13 | B 9 | C 63 | D 90 |

2 My number is made up of 5 tens and 7 ones.

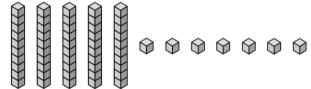

What is my number?

| A 75 | B 57 | C 12 | D 50 |

3 Which of these numbers has 7 tens?

| A 70 | B 7 | C 67 | D All of them |

4

Tens	Ones

Tens	Ones

Choose the correct statement.

| A 54 < 48 | B 48 > 54 | C 48 < 54 | D 48 = 54 |

5 Which does **not** show a bond to 100?

A 70 + 30 = 100

C 100 = 40 + 60

B 50 + 50 = 100

D 10 + 0 = 100

Think!

Complete the target number grid.

Target number of 75

Make it	Describe it 75 is made up of _____ _____	Break it apart 	Draw it

Why not try it with different target numbers?

These words might help you.

more   less

tens   ones

→ Practice book 1C p98

Unit 17
Time

In this unit we will …
- ⚡ Say if things happen before or after
- ⚡ Use a calendar
- ⚡ Tell time to the hour and the half hour
- ⚡ Compare time
- ⚡ Solve time word problems

This is a calendar. Can you use it to find how many days are in a week?

We will need some maths words. You may know some of these.

before   after   yesterday

today   tomorrow   day   week

slower   faster   month   year

calendar   date   minute hand

hour hand   o'clock   half past

second   minute   hour

There are lots of different types of clock. Do all of these show the same time?

Using before and after

Discover

1 **a)** What does Maya do **before** school?

b) What does Maya do **after** school?

Share

a)

I can point to the first picture of school and look at the pictures that come before it.

I will think about the things that I do before and after I go to school every day.

BEFORE SCHOOL

Before school:
- Maya wakes up.
- She gets dressed for school.
- She eats her breakfast.
- She brushes her teeth.
- She walks to school.

b)

AFTER SCHOOL

After school:
- Maya leaves school.
- She plays outside.
- She goes to bed and reads a book.

141

Think together

1 Point to what happens **before** and **after** Joe plays football.

2 Say what happens **before** and **after**.

I. BEFORE

2.

3. AFTER

3

Sunday

Monday

Tuesday

Wednesday

Thursday

Friday

Saturday

Can you use **yesterday**, **today** and **tomorrow** to talk about the weather?

a) What was the weather like before Tuesday?

b) What was the weather like on the day after Wednesday?

143

→ Practice book 1C p100

Using a calendar

Discover

This is my birthday!

I **a)** When is Aisha's birthday?

b) On what **day** of the **week** does Aisha visit the dentist? What **date** is this?

Share

a)

I can see the days of the week and numbers on the **calendar**. This will help me to read the date.

I wonder what time of **year** it is. How can you tell?

The calendar shows that Aisha's birthday is on a Sunday in the **month** of November.

It has a number 19 in the square, so the date is Sunday 19 November.

			November			
S	M	T	W	T	F	S
			1	2	3	4
5	6	7	8	9	10	11
12	13	14	15	16	17	18
19	20	21	22	23	24	25
	27	28	29	30		

b) Aisha visits the dentist on a Monday.

It is 13 November.

			November			
S	M	T	W	T	F	S
			1	2	3	4
5	6	7	8	9	10	11
12	13	14	15	16	17	18
19	20	21	22	23	24	25
	27	28	29	30		

Think together

1 When is Charlie's birthday?

Think about:
– the month
– the number day in the month
– the day of the week.

2

I am going horse riding on 8 July.

Izzy wants to draw a to show when she is going horse riding.

Point to where Izzy should put the ✖.

How many Mondays are in June?

CHALLENGE

January						
S	M	T	W	T	F	S
1	2	3	4	5	6	7
8	9	10	11	12	13	14
15	16	17	18	19	20	21
22	23	24	25	26	27	28
29	30	31				

February						
S	M	T	W	T	F	S
			1	2	3	4
5	6	7	8	9	10	11
12	13	14	15	16	17	18
19	20	21	22	23	24	25
26	27	28				

March						
S	M	T	W	T	F	S
			1	2	3	4
5	6	7	8	9	10	11
12	13	14	15	16	17	18
19	20	21	22	23	24	25
26	27	28	29	30	31	

April						
S	M	T	W	T	F	S
						1
2	3	4	5	6	7	8
9	10	11	12	13	14	15
16	17	18	19	20	21	22
23	24	25	26	27	28	29
30						

May						
S	M	T	W	T	F	S
	1	2	3	4	5	6
7	8	9	10	11	12	13
14	15	16	17	18	19	20
21	22	23	24	25	26	27
28	29	30	31			

June						
S	M	T	W	T	F	S
				1	2	3
4	5	6	7	8	9	10
11	12	13	14	15	16	17
18	19	20	21	22	23	24
25	26	27	28	29	30	

July						
S	M	T	W	T	F	S
						1
2	3	4	5	6	7	8
9	10	11	12	13	14	15
16	17	18	19	20	21	22
23	24	25	26	27	28	29
30	31					

August						
S	M	T	W	T	F	S
		1	2	3	4	5
6	7	8	9	10	11	12
13	14	15	16	17	18	19
20	21	22	23	24	25	26
27	28	29	30	31		

September						
S	M	T	W	T	F	S
					1	2
3	4	5	6	7	8	9
10	11	12	13	14	15	16
17	18	19	20	21	22	23
24	25	26	27	28	29	30

October						
S	M	T	W	T	F	S
1	2	3	4	5	6	7
8	9	10	11	12	13	14
15	16	17	18	19	20	21
22	23	24	25	26	27	28
29	30	31				

November						
S	M	T	W	T	F	S
			1	2	3	4
5	6	7	8	9	10	11
12	13	14	15	16	17	18
19	20	21	22	23	24	25
26	27	28	29	30		

December						
S	M	T	W	T	F	S
					1	2
3	4	5	6	7	8	9
10	11	12	13	14	15	16
17	18	19	20	21	22	23
24	25	26	27	28	29	30
31						

There is so much you can tell from a calendar. It shows us how many days are in each month. It also tells us when each date is.

→ Practice book 1C p103

Telling time to the hour

Discover

1 **a)** What time does the clock say?

b) The party starts at 5 o'clock.

What will the clock show?

Share

a)

> There are two hands on a clock. I wonder what the difference between them is.

The longer hand is the **minute hand**. When it points to 12, it shows an **o'clock** time.

The shorter hand is the **hour hand**. This tells us the **hour** that it is.

The clock says that the time is 3 o'clock.

> I now know how to draw other o'clock times.

b) The hour hand will point to 5 and the minute hand will point to 12.

> I wonder how long there is between o'clock times.

Think together

1 What time is it?

The time is ☐ o'clock.

2 What time is it?

The time is ☐ o'clock.

3 What mistake has each child made?

I have drawn 10 o'clock.

I have drawn 4 o'clock.

Paul

Maria

Paul has _____

_____ .

Maria has _____

_____ .

Telling time to the half hour

Discover

Assembly is at **half past** 10. Will you remind me?

1 **a)** What time is it now?

b) What will the clock look like when it is time for assembly?

Share

a) The minute hand is halfway around the clock. It is pointing to the number 6.

When the minute hand points to 6, it shows a half-past time.

At half-past times, always look at the number that the hour hand has moved halfway past.

The hour hand is halfway between the 9 and 10. I think that means the time is halfway between 9 o'clock and 10 o'clock.

The time is half past 9.

b) Assembly is at half past 10.

The clock will look like this:

I used my finger to trace the clock hands at half past 10.

153

Think together

1 What time is it?

The time is half past ⬜.

2 What time is it?

The time is _____

_____ .

3

I have drawn half past 8.

I have drawn half past 2.

Sidra

Filip

What mistake has each child made?

Sidra has _____

_____

Filip has _____

_____

I am going to draw what each clock should look like.

155

Writing time

Discover

I **a)** We can use a clock to measure how long activities take. What do we use to measure time?

b) Estimate how long you think it will take:

- to walk along the
- to run around the
- to paint the .

Share

a) There are 60 **seconds** in I **minute**.

There are 60 minutes in I hour.
All clocks have a minute hand.
It takes 60 minutes to move all
the way around.

I second   60 seconds

> My clock has a second
> hand so I can count to
> 60 as it moves around.
> Not all clocks have a
> second hand.

I minute   60 minutes

Time is measured in seconds, minutes and hours.

> How long does
> a second, a minute
> or an hour feel?

> We have to learn
> from experience how
> to estimate time.

b) I estimate:

- walking along the  might take seconds

- running around the  might take minutes

- painting the  might take hours.

Think together

1 How long do you think it would take to do ten star jumps?

Would it take seconds, minutes or hours?

2 Would you measure these activities in minutes?

| Reading a book | Writing your name | Playing outside |

3 **a)**

How long does it take you to say the alphabet?

A, B, C, D...

I will measure this in _____ .

It takes me ☐ _____ to say the alphabet.

b)

How long does it take you to read five pages of a book?

I will use a timer to measure how long it takes.

I will measure this in _____ .

It takes me ☐ _____ to read five pages of a book.

159

→ Practice book 1C p112

Comparing time

Discover

> Yesterday it took us 20 minutes to tidy the whole classroom. Can we all tidy more quickly today, please?

> I tidied my desk in I minute yesterday.

George

1 **a)** What time would be **faster** than 20 minutes to tidy the classroom?

b) If George tidies his desk in 30 seconds today, is this faster or **slower** than I minute?

Share

I will use 20 🧊 to represent 20 minutes.

a) If we make a chain that is longer than 20 🧊 it is a greater number. A greater number of 🧊 than 20 means the task takes more time than 20 minutes so it is slower. A smaller number means it takes less time and is faster.

20 minutes

21 minutes

21 is greater than 20.

So 21 minutes is slower than 20 minutes.

Now I will make a chain with a smaller number than 20 🧊.

20 minutes

19 minutes

19 is less than 20.

So 19 minutes is faster than 20 minutes.

Tidying the classroom in 19 minutes would be faster.

I wonder if there are any other times that are faster than 20 minutes.

b) 60 seconds

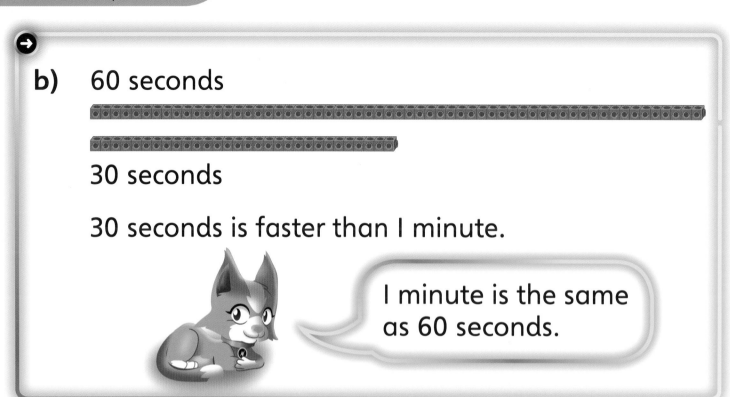

30 seconds

30 seconds is faster than I minute.

I minute is the same as 60 seconds.

Think together

1 Who painted faster?

I took 18 minutes to paint this!

Izzy

James

I took 24 minutes to paint this!

18 minutes

24 minutes

☐ minutes is faster than ☐ minutes.

_____ painted faster.

2 Compare the 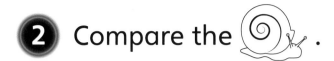 .

Use the correct word in each sentence.

I took 7 hours!

I took 4 hours!

7 is a **smaller / greater** number than 4.

7 hours is **more time / less time** than 4 hours.

7 hours is **longer / shorter** than 4 hours.

One snail took 7 hours. This is **faster / slower** than 4 hours.

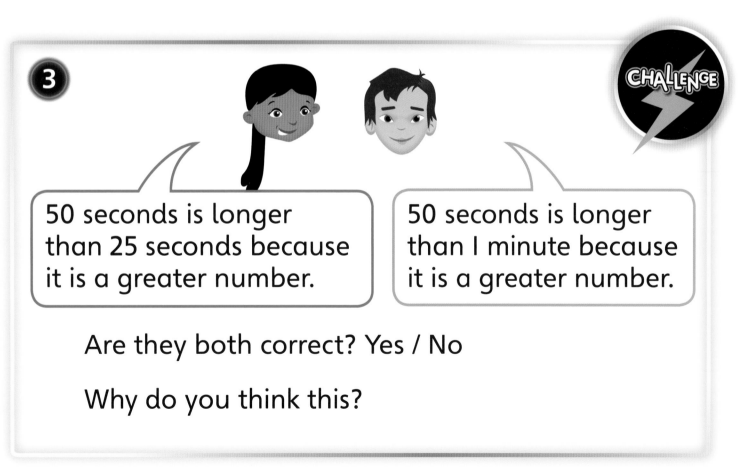

3

CHALLENGE

50 seconds is longer than 25 seconds because it is a greater number.

50 seconds is longer than 1 minute because it is a greater number.

Are they both correct? Yes / No

Why do you think this?

163

→ Practice book 1C p115

Solving word problems – time

Discover

5 minutes   3 minutes

1 **a)** How long does it take to cook a  ?

    b) It takes 2 minutes less to make a

       than a .

       How long does it take to make a ?

Share

I used a number line to help.

a)

I know my bonds. I know that 5 + 3 = 8.
It is a fact I have learned.

It takes 8 minutes to cook a  .

b) It took 8 minutes to cook a .

It takes 2 minutes less to make a .

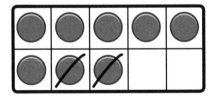

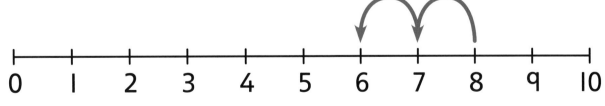

8 − 2 = 6

It takes 6 minutes to make a .

Think together

1 Zac cooks a 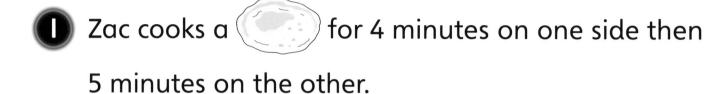 for 4 minutes on one side then 5 minutes on the other.

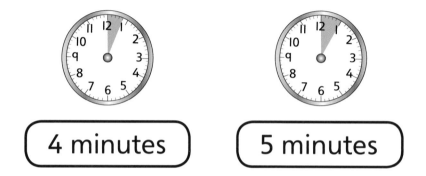

4 minutes   5 minutes

How long does Zac take to cook his  ?

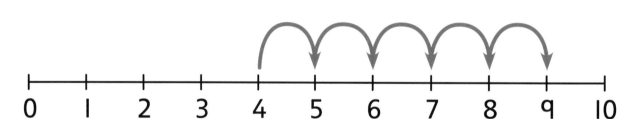

0   1   2   3   4   5   6   7   8   9   10

4 + 5 = ☐

Zac takes ☐ minutes to cook his .

2 It takes Hassan 2 minutes to run from one cone to the other. He does this 7 times.

2 minutes

2 minutes

Abbie does the same activity. Her total time is 3 minutes less than Hassan's total.

How long does Abbie take?

First, I will work out how long Hassan takes altogether by counting in 2s.

Hassan takes ☐ minutes altogether.

Now I need to take away 3 to find the answer.

Abbie takes ☐ minutes.

167

→ Practice book 1C p118

End of unit check

Your teacher will ask you these questions.

1 The month after March is

_____ .

A February   C April

B May   D June

2 Harry's birthday is on 25 July.

What day of the week is Harry's birthday?

A Tuesday   C Thursday

B Friday   D Saturday

3 Which clock is showing 9 o'clock?

A    B    C    D

4 Harry goes to bed at this time.

Mia goes to bed **2** hours later.

What time does Mia go to bed?

A	half past 7		C	half past 9
B	9 o'clock		D	half past 5

5 Hamza takes 24 minutes to climb a hill.

Ellie takes 21 minutes.

Which sentence is true?

A Hamza is faster than Ellie.

B Hamza takes less time than Ellie.

C Ellie takes more time than Hamza.

D Ellie is faster than Hamza.

Think!

Look at these two clocks.
What's the same? What's different?

These words
might help you.

minute hand

hour hand

half past

169

→ Practice book 1C p121

Unit 18
Money

In this unit we will …
- ⚡ Learn about coins
- ⚡ Learn about notes
- ⚡ Count in 1s, 2s, 5s and 10s using coins

Here are some coins. Do you know which is the 5 pence coin?

Have you heard these money words before? Which letter means pence?

pound   pence

coins   notes   p

Do you remember these signs? > < Complete this sentence using > or < .

Recognising coins

Discover

Before   After

1 **a)** Which coins are in the tray to start with?

b) Which coin has been removed from the tray?

Key 1p 2p 5p 10p 20p 50p £1 £2

Share

The number on the coin tells us how much the coin is worth.

a)

There is a:

 1 pence coin

 2 pence coin

 5 pence coin

 10 pence coin

 20 pence coin

 50 pence coin

 1 pound coin

 2 pound coin

I wonder what is different between a 1 pence coin and a 1 pound coin.

b)

The has been removed from the tray.

Think together

1

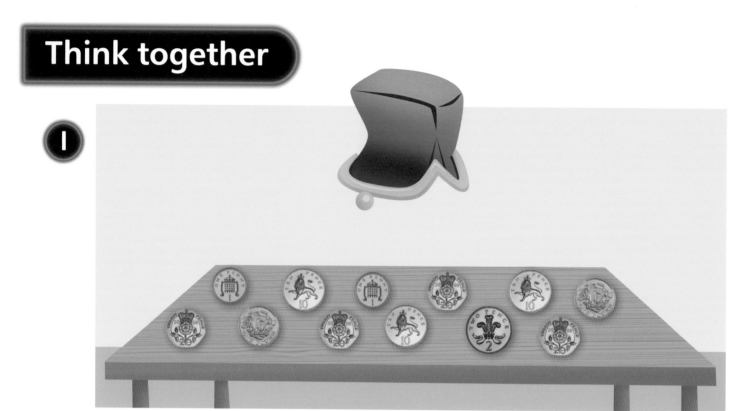

Which coins can you see?

Copy and complete the table.

Coin	How many?
1 pence	
2 pence	
5 pence	
10 pence	
20 pence	
50 pence	
1 pound	
2 pound	

Key 1p 2p 5p 10p 20p 50p £1   £2

2

Complete the sentences.

a) The 1 pence coin is to the left of the _____ .

b) The _____ coin is to the right of the 50 pence coin.

c) The 50 pence coin is to the _____ of the 2 pound coin.

3 Complete the sentences.

CHALLENGE

Write the value of the coins.

Then choose > (greater than) than or < (less than).

a) ◎ ☐ pence is ◯ ◎ ☐ pence.

b) ◎ ☐ pence is ◯ ◎ ☐ pence.

c) ◎ ☐ pence is ◯ ◎ ☐ pound.

How could I describe a 20 pence coin?

 £5 £10 £20 £50

→ Practice book 1C p123

Recognising notes

Discover

1 **a)** What notes can you see?

b) Put the notes in order from least to greatest.

Key 1p 2p 5p 10p 20p 50p £1 £2

Share

a)

There are some:

 5 pound notes

 10 pound notes

 20 pound notes

 50 pound notes

The number on the note tells us what it is worth.

b)

least ⟶ greatest

Think together

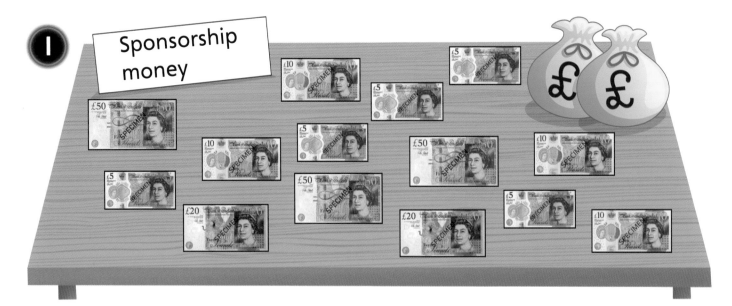

Sponsorship money

Count the notes.

Copy and complete the table.

Note	How many?
£5	
£10	
£20	
£50	

Key 1p 2p 5p 10p 20p 50p £1 £2

2 Match the note to the correct words.

10 pounds

50 pounds

20 pounds

5 pounds

3 Use < or > to complete the sentences.

 CHALLENGE

a) ◯

b)  ◯

c)  ◯

 £5 £10 £20 £50

→ Practice book 1C p126

Counting with coins

Discover

1 **a)** How much money is in each line?

b) Which line has the most coins?

Which line has the most money?

Key 1p 2p 5p 10p 20p 50p £1 £2

Share

a)

 I counted the coins.

There are five 1 pence coins.

1, 2, 3, 4, 5

There is 5 pence altogether.

There are four 2 pence coins.

2, 4, 6, 8

There is 8 pence altogether.

There are six 5 pence coins.

5, 10, 15, 20, 25, 30

There is 30 pence altogether.

There are four 10 pence coins.

10, 20, 30, 40

There is 40 pence altogether.

b) The most coins are in the 5 pence line.

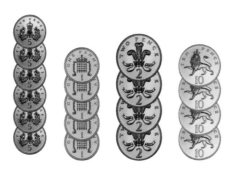

Why is the line with the most coins not the line with the most money?

The most money is in the 10 pence line.

Think together

1 How much do the coins make altogether?

a)

There is ☐ pence in total.

b)

There is ☐ pence in total.

c)

There is ☐ pence in total.

Key 1p 2p 5p 10p 20p 50p £1 £2

2 Work out how much the coins in each group make.
Then put >, < or = between them.

a)

b)

c)

3 Sidra has 15 pence.

All her coins are the same.

Which of these coins does she have?

Explain your answer.

 £5   £10 £20   £50

→ Practice book 1C p129

End of unit check

Your teacher will ask you these questions.

1 Which coin is worth 20 pence?

A    B    C    D

2 Which one is worth five pounds?

A   B   C    D

3 How much money is here altogether?

A 2 pence   **B** 10 pence   **C** 5 pence   **D** 8 pence

4 Which coin is **less than** 10 pence?

  A   B   C   D

5 Which is not a real coin or note?

A   B   C  D

Think!

How many ways can you make 20 pence using ,

 and ?

You can use each coin more than once.

These words might help you.

pence   coin

five   ten   two

is equal to

185

→ Practice book 1C p132

I am proud of how much we have learned this year!

I know! We can do anything if we practise!

Holiday fun

Here are some ideas you can try at home.

Practise sorting

Find 10 toys. Sort them into two groups and cover one group with a blanket.

How many are left? _____

Can you work out how many are under the blanket?

_____

Find 3D shapes

Look for 3D shapes at home!

What can you find that is a cube? _____

Where can you find a cuboid? _____

How many cylinders can you find? _____

Can you find any other 3D shapes? Draw them!

Tell the time

What time did you eat lunch each day this week?

Monday _____   Friday _____

Tuesday _____   Saturday _____

Wednesday _____   Sunday _____

Thursday _____

Do you always eat lunch at the same time?

Speedy counting

See how quickly you can count from 1 to 100.

Can you count backwards from 100?

Try it with a friend to see who is quickest!

Play 'Secret Number'

Think of a number between 1 and 20. Keep it secret!

Your friend has to guess your secret number. He or she gets five guesses.

Help your friend by saying if your number is greater than or less than the number they guess.

It is always good to learn new things!

What we have learned

Can you do all these things?

- ⚡ Count in 10s, 5s and 2s
- ⚡ Make arrays
- ⚡ Find halves and quarters
- ⚡ Describe position and direction
- ⚡ Work with numbers up to 100
- ⚡ Use a calendar and start to tell the time
- ⚡ Count with coins and notes

Now you are ready to continue your maths journey in Year 2!